Dog Pub Walks
Peak District

Wet Nose
Publishing Ltd

www.countrysidedogwalks.co.uk

First published in April 2018 by **Wet Nose Publishing Ltd**
All enquiries regarding sales telephone: 01824 704398
email cdw@wetnosepublishing.co.uk
www.countrysidedogwalks.co.uk
ISBN 978-0-9931923-8-8

Upper Derwent
Reservoirs

Ladybower
Reservoir

Shef

A57

1 **2** **3**

4 **5** **8**

6 **7**

A623

9

A619

A6 **10**

11

12

A515 **13**

14 Matloc

15

Contents

Introduction

The walks included in this book are all designed so that you and your wet-nosed friend have a really enjoyable time. Where there are stiles, they are specially designed with lift gates for dogs. At a quick glance there is information at the beginning of each walk to tell you what to expect and what you may need to take with you. The descriptive guides will also warn of any roads ahead or areas of livestock so that you can get your dog on the lead well in advance.

Dogs just love to explore new places. They really enjoy the new smells and carry themselves a little higher with the added excitement. Going to new places gets you and your dog out and about, meeting new people and their dogs. It is important to socialise dogs, as they will be more likely to act in a friendly manner towards other dogs as they gain confidence.

The stunning pictures in this book are just a taster of what you can see along the way. Many of the walks have fantastic views and scenery. Some of the walks are wooded, offering shade on those hot summer days.

The walks are graded Easy, Medium and Challenging. They are all around one to three hours long, depending on your and your dog's pace. You may start with the easy ones and work up to the challenging walks depending on your and your dog's fitness. Different dog breeds and dog age must be taken into account when you decide which walks to do.

Different breeds of dog have different levels of fitness. For example, bulldogs can only do short walks, whereas a border collie or a springer spaniel are extremely energetic and difficult to tire out. It is recommended that you do some research on the breed of dog that you own, to help you know what sort of exercise that they require.

You may have a walk that you are happy doing with your dog every day, but this book will show you new areas to explore with a change of scenery and a chance to meet new people and their dogs. Dogs love new places to visit and you will see the change in them as they explore the new surroundings, taking

in the new smells with delight. You will fulfil both your life and your dog's just by trying somewhere new.

Some of the walks include bridleways, so you may encounter horses and cyclists. It is important to put your dog on a lead if you see horses approach. It is always helpful to say hello to the riders as they draw near, so that the horse realises that you are not a threat.

The Peak District National Park

In 1951, the Peak District was the first area in the UK to be designated as a National Park. It lies in central and northern England, mainly in Derbyshire but covering small areas of Staffordshire, South and West Yorkshire, Cheshire and Greater Manchester.

The majority of land within the National Park is privately owned, consisting mostly of agricultural land. The National Trust own 12%, and the National Park Authority own 5%, several water companies are also major land owners; however the National Park Authority oversees land management throughout the park, and planning restrictions protect the area from inappropriate development and land use.

The north (Dark Peak) and south (White Peak) differ greatly. The north is dominated by vast open moorland, with several reservoirs and forest plantations. The exposed bedrock is mostly gritstone which is dark in colour, which can be seen throughout, with many cliff faces, rock stacks and rock formations. The south has many dales and steep-sided natural woodland, with rivers flowing through the bottom. The bedrock is mostly limestone, which is white in colour and is also highly visible with many cliff faces rising up from the valley floor.

Visitors to the National Park would be forgiven for thinking that they are miles from any town or city, but in fact the cities of Manchester and Sheffield lie on the boundaries, sandwiching the National Park in the middle.

Ground Nesting Birds

Watch out for vulnerable ground nesting birds from early March until the end of July. Dogs that stray off the main paths may disturb birds and chicks, possibly killing them or breaking eggs. Species to look out for are Skylarks, Meadow pipits, Curlew, Red and Black grouse, Snipe and Pheasants.

Some if not all of these birds are declining in numbers, due partly to their vulnerability when nesting. Dogs are a threat to them, even if treading on them unintentionally. Some other threats are foxes, badgers, stoats, weasels, birds of prey and crows.

Please help to protect these birds during the nesting season by keeping your dog on the paths when walking in open areas such as grassland, moors, heathland and scrub.

Rivers

Some dogs love water and will think nothing of plunging into the river. With the extreme weather conditions over the last few years, a river that may be safe for your dog to swim in can change in a matter of hours to become a swollen torrent that could wash your dog away. Please be careful when near rivers if there have been heavy periods of rain or if they look swollen or fast flowing. It is best to put your dogs on the lead, until you have assessed the situation.

Livestock

If you find that you need to cross a field with cattle or horses and they seem interested in you or your dog, it is recommended within the Countryside Code to let your dog off the lead. Never try to get between livestock and your dog. Your dog will get out of a situation a lot more easily with speed than you can. It is usually only cattle with young calves that are a threat, or young heifers or bullocks that tend to get a little inquisitive. They will usually stop when they get close to you or your dog.

Most horses will come over for a fuss but a small proportion do have a problem with dogs. They may see them as a threat and will act to defend the herd. Horses that are out with a rider are completely different as they are not defending the herd, and as long as you keep a safe distance there should not be a problem.

Sheep are not a danger to you, but your dog can be a danger to them. Where sheep are grazing it is vital that you have your dog on a lead or under very close control. You will know your dog, but if you are unsure it is better to play safe and keep your dog on a lead. It is important always to have your dog on a lead when around lambs. Lambs have a higher pitched bleat and can be the size of a cat, and your dog may act differently amongst them.

Pub Etiquette

All the pubs featured in this book welcome you and your dog, so you can relax part way around or at the end of a good walk. Dogs must be kept on a lead whilst inside the pub and we would ask that you consider other people. For instance, please don't allow your dog to lie down in the doorways or in thoroughfares. In wet weather, avoid your dog shaking his coat where he may spray mud onto people, which is not very pleasant, especially if they are eating. Remember, not all people like dogs, and some people may be allergic to them, or even frightened of them. If you consider this before going in it will help towards ensuring that the pub that you are visiting stays dog-friendly. **Please Note:** we recommend you telephone in advance to check opening times and to book in advance for meals.

Does your dog fetch a stick?

Most dogs love sticks and will pick them up without any encouragement from their owners. Vets and dog trainers recommend that you should not throw sticks for dogs. They can cause nasty injuries, sometimes fatal as the stick can pierce the throat, or rebound off the ground and cause harm to your dog.

Ticks

If you have been walking in areas where sheep graze, you should check your dog for ticks. They must be removed as soon as possible. It is best to use tick tweezers, which are specially designed to remove the head and leg parts of the tick. Ticks can carry diseases and the longer they remain latched on to your dog the more the chance of spreading infections.

Dogs and Alcohol

Please note: alcohol is poisonous to dogs!

Throughout this book there are jokes about dogs drinking alcohol, this is intended as humour by humanising dogs in funny situations. Any dog pictured drinking beer is only supping alcohol-free drinks and it must be stressed that dogs should never be given alcohol.

Please clean up after your dog

Always be prepared, having dog bags with you at all times. Once you have cleaned up after your dog, please keep the bag, until you see a bin. If there are no bins provided, then take it away with you to a roadside bin. Dog bags that are discarded on the paths or in the bushes are unpleasant and unsightly, and will not degrade.

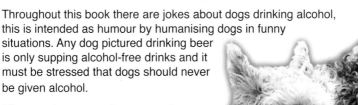

"Aaaah, a well earned pint at last!"

1. Edale - The Old Nags Head pub

Tel: 01433 670291   Challenging - 7 miles - 4hr

This is a wonderful walk, through open countryside, beginning in the Grinds Brook valley. There is some easy scrambling as you ascend out of the valley, but if you are nimble on your feet you won't need to use your hands. The walk was done with a West Highland terrier, who managed the walk without any help over the rocks. After your ascent you will cross the moors. Boulders are strewn across the landscape and have wonderful formations, some of which look like giant mushrooms. There may be livestock throughout the walk. There may be ground nesting birds on the moors. **Do not attempt to do this walk in winter, as the paths are very boggy and clouds may close in, making visibility very poor.**

How to get there – On reaching Edale, follow the sign for the train station. Continue under the railway bridge (ignoring the final turn off for the station), and at the end of the road you will reach the pub and parking bay.

Grid Reference – SK 122 860   **Postcode** – S33 7ZD

Parking – Park at the side of the road in front of the pub. There's further parking near to the train station, which is a pay and display

Facilities – None

You will need – Dog leads, dog bags and water in hot weather

The Walk

❶ With the pub in front of you, continue straight ahead on the quiet road, and pass the gable end of the pub on your right. Continue on the access road, beside the houses. Follow the sign on the fingerpost to Grindsbrook. Ascend on a lane between stone walls. On reaching 'The Lodge' on your left, turn right, following the sign on the fingerpost for Grindsbrook.

Descend the steps, and then cross a footbridge over a river. Put your dog on a lead, or under close control, as there may be livestock grazing. Pass through a gate and ascend on the cobbled steps into farmland. Continue on the stone slab path and ignore the footpath on your right, which ascends across the field.

You will pass a wide gap in the stone wall, where you enter into another field. At the end of the field, you will reach and pass through a gate into a wood. Continue on the path. At the end of the wood, put your dog on a lead or under close control and pass through a gate.

Cross a beautifully crafted footbridge over a stream, where your dog can get a drink. Continue straight ahead into open countryside, with a river (Grinds Brook) below on your left. Ascend gently on the obvious path as you continue into the valley. You will ascend a little steeper as you continue. There are some interesting rock formations ahead and on your right.

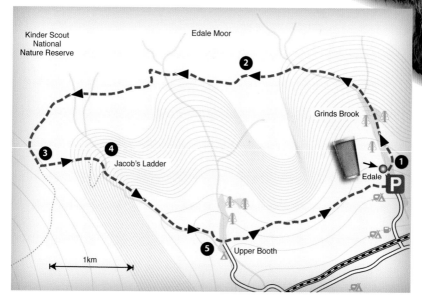

You will reach a rocky section. Veer a little to your right, and choose your route around the rocks, but stay close to them, and when you can, veer back over to your left. You will see well-worn paths as you continue. Keep heading into the valley, with the river below on your left.

You will have some rocks to step over as you go. As you veer over to your left, you will see an obvious path. Continue on the path, where you will reach level with the river. Ascend again, where you will climb over some rocks. You will reach a fence line. Pass through a gate, and continue beside the river.

When you reach a steep scree slope on your right the path runs out. Cross the river via the stones. Continue in the same direction, heading upstream of the river. Stay close to the river, which has now narrowed to a stream. This section of path has lots of rock to step up onto.

As you continue, the stream veers sharply to your right and you will see a cutting on your left. Ascend into the cutting, climbing the rocks as you climb out of the valley, close to a small stream (which may dry up). As you near the top of the cutting, the stream veers to your right. Keep to your left.

You will reach another path as you leave the cutting. Cross this path, and continue straight ahead on a stone slab path. Continue on this path for some distance across the moor. On reaching a rock formation continue straight ahead, ignoring the stone slab path on your left. At times the stone slabs end, where you will cross natural rock under foot, and exposed soil. Continue in the same direction on the worn path.

As you continue, you will descend into a gully. Keep to your right a little here, as the path is less steep, and you may have to cross a stream after periods of rain. Ignore the paths left and right, and continue straight ahead, where you will ascend out of the gully on the cobble path. At first keep the rock formations on your left. Soon after the rock formations increase, and you will walk between them. The route isn't clear here, but keep going in the same direction, staying near, but not too close to the slope on your left. ❷ You will reach the familiar stone slab path in places, where you cross over the moor between the rocks. You will pass small cairns (piles of stone).

After some distance you will reach a large cairn, which is about 6ft high. Pass the cairn on your right and continue straight ahead, where you will ascend on a slab path. When the slab path ends, continue on a cobbled path, which will veer ahead and left. Continue on the path as you descend towards a stone wall in the distance. A little further along the path will become stone slab once again.

❸ Continue on the slab path as it veers to your left, ignoring the path on your right, which leads to the stone wall. You will begin to descend into the valley once again. You will reach and continue close to a stock fence on your right.

You will descend a little more steeply on a cobble stone path. As you pass a stone post on your left, you will descend on a sunken path.

❹ On reaching another cairn and a waymarker, take the path on your left, which is marked Pennine Way. You will begin a steep descent, with rough steps known as Jacob's ladder. At the bottom of the steps you will reach and cross a lovely stone bridge.

Go through a gate and continue on the path. You will reach and pass through another gate, beside a stile. Continue on the path beside a stone wall on your left and cross a sloped field. On reaching the end of the field, go through another gate beside a stile. Continue straight ahead on the edge of another sloping field, and continue with the stone wall on your left.

As you continue a stock fence takes the place of the stone wall. You will pass some silver birch trees on your right. Put your dog on a lead as you descend towards the farm building. Go between the farm buildings and pass through a gate. Pass a farmhouse on your left and continue to descend on the access road.

Ignore a footpath on your right and continue on the road. Ignore a footpath on your left and then cross a bridge over the river. **❺** Just after, turn left following the sign on the fingerpost for Edale and enter into a farmyard. Cross the farmyard, and then turn right. As you leave the farmyard, ignore a footpath straight ahead, and continue between stone walls. Just after, turn right on the lane following the sign 'Footpath to Edale'. Continue between the stone walls and then pass between some old gate posts and continue on the track between stock fences.

On reaching a gate, put your dog on a lead or under close control, and pass through it. Continue on the edge of a field, beside a stock fence on your left. Continue on the path, where you will veer to your right. Pass between stone posts and then veer to your left on the obvious worn path.

Go through a gate and enter another field. Continue on the obvious worn path, which cuts out the corner of the field. Ascend close to a stock fence on your right. Pass through a gate and continue to ascend on the obvious worn path, where you will pass between hillocks. On reaching a stone wall, pass through the gate and continue straight ahead on fairly level ground. You will have wonderful views on your right and straight ahead. Continue in the same direction, where you will cross over several fields, the latter fields have a slab path.

On entering into the fifth and final field, you will reach a finger post. Turn right and follow the sign for Pennine Way. Shortly after, pass through another gate and continue between fences and banks, with a stream on your left. Descend gradually, and then continue between houses. On reaching the road, you will be back at the car park and pub.

2. Mam Tor - The Rambler Inn

Tel: 01433 670 268   Challenging - 4.8 miles - 3hr

This circular walk has outstanding panoramic views, and a clear day is a must. You will cross farmland, and there are some quiet lanes, before reaching the valley and village of Edale. Continue through farmland and quiet lanes, where you will ascend to Hollins Cross. Here you can walk on the good path along the ridge, with spectacular views into valleys on either side, until you reach Mam Tor. There are sheep grazing for roughly half the walk and there are cattle on a small section. The cattle show no interest, as walkers are frequent in the area (read the advice in the introduction under the heading Cattle). There are sections of quiet roads with no pavements. You will reach the pub in about an hour.

How to get there – From Chapel en le Frith take the Sheffield Road, following the sign for Edale. As you continue on the road ignore the left turn signed for Edale and Barber Booth, and continue on the road. You will find the car park on your left soon after.

Grid Reference – SK 123832

Parking – Pay and Display in the National Trust Mam Tor car park

Facilities – None

You will need – Dog leads, dog bags

The Walk

1 From the car park, keep to the left hand side and ascend away from the road, you will see a set of steps. Ensure that you have your dog on a lead, as you will be walking beside a road. Ascend the steps and continue on the path, parallel with the road on your left.

When you reach the road, go through a kissing gate straight ahead of you and ascend the steps where you will soon have views to your right looking across Hope Valley. As you rise a little higher you will have views across the Edale Valley on your left.

Continue straight ahead when the main path veers to your right away from the road. Continue on the narrow path beside the stock fence and the road. You will reach a gate and a bus stop on your left. Don't go through the gate, but you will see two paths ahead. Take the path ahead and left, where you will descend. You will leave the road behind. Pass through a gate and then descend beside a stone wall, with a grass slope on your right.

There are wonderful views ahead and to your left. Continue on the path, which veers away from the stone wall. You will reach and continue beside a stock fence. Soon after, pass through a gate and continue between fences. You will pass a house on your left near the end of the path.

On reaching a gate pass though it, put your dog on a lead and descend a short distance and pass through the gate on your left, following the sign on

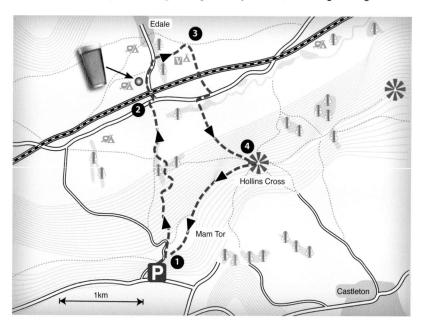

the fingerpost for Edale. Descend on the quiet road, and ignore a footpath on your left. Pass a farmyard and house on your left.

After a road bridge you will reach a busy road. ❷ Turn right on this road, and then take the first road on your left. Pass a car park on your right and cross the head of a road on your left. Continue straight ahead, where you will pass under a railway bridge.

Just after, you will reach 'The Rambler Inn' on your left. On leaving the pub, turn left on the road. Pass 'The Moorland Centre' on your right and just after, take the footpath on your right. Descend between stone walls. Cross a bridge over a river, and pass through a small gate and then between squeeze stones. There may be sheep grazing, so keep your dog under close control or on a lead.

Ignore a footpath immediately on your right and continue straight ahead, on the edge of a field. On reaching a gate, pass through the small gate and continue on the edge of a field, beside a stone wall on your right. There are views in all directions, and you are surrounded by distant hills.

You will reach a small gate, put your dog on a lead, go through the gate and enter into a farmyard. Continue straight ahead and cross the farmyard. Veer to your right and pass houses on your left and right. You will leave the farmyard, and reach a quiet road. ❸ Turn right and descend on the road, where you can enjoy the views.

At the end of the road turn right. Pass a derelict building on your right. Soon after you will pass a house on your left and a track. Take the footpath on your left immediately after the track. Go through a gate and descend on the track between fences. You will cross a bridge over a river, and then pass through a small gate. Keep your dog under close control or on a lead, as there may be sheep and cattle grazing. Continue straight ahead and ascend on the track between hillocks. There is a stream on your right, where your dog can get a drink. Continue on the track as it weaves across the hillside.

You will pass a stone barn on your right, and continue straight ahead. You will reach and continue beside a barbed wire fence on your right, with a gully beyond it. Just after you pass the gully, turn right following the sign on the fingerpost for Hollins Cross.

Ascend across a sloped field and then ascend a set of steps. Pass through a gate into open countryside. Continue on a short boardwalk and then veer to your right and ascend the hill on the worn path.

"Waste not, want not!"

As you continue, the path will become sunken between banks. Ascend between patches of gorse. Near the top your path will merge with another from your right. Continue to ascend a little steeper.

❹ On reaching a pillar/memorial (Hollins Cross) and another path, which is surfaced with stone flags, you will have stunning panoramic views.

Turn right on the flagged path, where you will have a steady ascent until you reach the summit at Mam Tor. Before reaching Mam Tor you will pass through two gates, and as you do, continue straight ahead on the slab path. Ascend quite steeply, where you pass between hillocks. You will reach a trig point at the summit, where the views are quite stunning.

Continue straight ahead, and descend on the slab path, which has some steps. Ignore a path which veers to your right, and continue on the main path. You will reach a familiar spot. Put your dog on a lead and retrace your steps back to the car park.

3. Win Hill - The Yorkshire Bridge Inn

Tel: 01433 651361   Challenging - 4.2 miles - 2hr 30min

This is a brilliant circular walk, with some steep ascents in places until you reach the top of Win Hill. There are amazing panoramic views across Ladybower and over to Mam Tor, which make the ascent worthwhile. There may be sheep grazing for a large part of the walk, as you cross through moorland and farmland. There is a small section of road, and you will cross Yorkshire Bridge, where you can enjoy river views. The pub is located close to the end of the walk.

How to get there – From Hope valley follow the road towards Sheffield. Just as you enter into Bamford take the A6013 on your left, signed for Bamford. Continue through the village and a little further along the road, just before reaching the traffic lights, the car park will be on your right. From the A57 Snake Pass, on reaching the traffic lights turn onto the A6013 and the car park will be on the left.

Grid Reference – SK 202859   **Postcode** – S33 0BY

Parking – Pay and Display Heatherdene car park

Facilities – Toilets in the car park

You will need – Dog leads, dog bags

The Walk

❶ Keep your dog on a lead to begin this walk. From the car park, with your back to the road, go to the right hand side, follow the sign for 'pay and display'. Pass the pay and display on your left, where you will see a surfaced track. Take this track and pass the toilet block on your left. Pass through the gate and continue on this path, passing steps on your right. Continue between the trees and rhododendrons. When you see the dam wall on the right, take the next path on the right. Descend the steps to the main road. Cross the road, and keep your dog on a lead until you reach the end of the dam wall, as he/she may jump over thinking that it is level on the other side.

Follow the path across the dam. If you look over the wall at the beginning you will see up close the plughole-design drain, which lets the water flow from the reservoir. **❷** Once you have crossed the dam, pass through the gate and cross the tarmac path, ignore the left and right turn and ascend on the path that veers to your left. The path cuts across a wooded hillside. As you continue to ascend there is a ravine on your left and you will pass small waterfalls and a weir, where your dog can get a drink.

Ascend steeply beside the stream. On reaching another path, cross it and continue to ascend straight ahead. Leave the stream shortly afterwards. On reaching a stone wall and a stock fence, keep your dog under close control or on a lead as there may be livestock, and pass through a gate. Turn right, then immediately turn left, following the sign on the fingerpost for Win Hill.

Continue to ascend on the edge of a larch plantation. Ascend the steps into heathland. Ascend another set of steps. Continue straight ahead, as you pass through a gap in the stone wall. Ascend another set of steps, where you will reach the summit of Win Hill and a trig point. On a clear day, you will have fantastic panoramic views.

❸ Just after you pass the trig point, the easiest way down is by veering to your left. Descend the rocks to reach a path. Turn right and continue to descend. You will reach and continue beside a stock fence on your left. Look out for a kissing gate over on your left. On reaching this, don't go through the gate but stay on the path, and then shortly afterwards take the narrow path on your right.

Continue on the path, descending gently through the middle of the heather moorland. After you have crossed the moor you will reach a gate. Don't go

"Why does she always go into that room with 'Ladies' on it?"

through the gate, but continue on a path with a stone wall on your left, which is marked by a waymarker.

Continue on the path, where you will veer away from the stone wall. You will reach and continue beside a stock fence, where you will begin to ascend. On reaching a gate, pass through it and follow the sign on the fingerpost for Thornhill. Continue between a stock fence and a stone wall.

You will pass another fingerpost on your right, and continue straight ahead, following the sign for Thornhill. After you have passed a block of woodland on your left, you will have views into the valley. Continue beside a dilapidated stone wall on your right. The path will level out, and cut across a gently sloping hillside covered with heather and bracken.

As you continue, you will also have views ahead of you. You will pass a water trough on your right, and just after you will pass a fingerpost. Continue straight ahead and descend between heather covered banks. ❹ On reaching another fingerpost and a stone wall, turn left following the sign for Thronhill. Descend steeply, beside the stone wall on your right. On reaching a gate pass through it and continue to descend beside the stone wall, with scrub on your left.

Continue on the path between scrub. On reaching a gate pass through it and continue straight ahead. Just before you reach a fingerpost and gate on your right, veer to your left and descend the steps, following the sign on the fingerpost for Yorkshire Bridge. Continue to descend between scrub. The path may be boggy after heavy rain.

You will reach an opening. Continue straight ahead on the well-worn grass path, as you cross a sloped field. Pass through a gap in the stone wall and continue across another field. At the end of the field, continue on the path beside scrub and trees. On reaching a fingerpost and a good surfaced path, turn left on the bridleway. Almost immediately turn right, and descend the steps. Continue to descend between scrub and trees. On reaching a gate, put your dog on a lead and go through the gate, where you will soon reach a quiet road.

Turn left on the road, with a river below on your right. You will reach and cross a bridge (Yorkshire Bridge), where you will have lovely views of the river and weir. After crossing the bridge, continue on this quiet road. You will reach a housing estate on your left. Take the third road on your left (Bemrose Gate). Continue with the houses on your left. At the end of the road, you will reach the main road and the Yorkshire Bridge Inn is on your left.

On leaving the pub, cross carefully over the road and turn left. Continue on the road, where you will reach a familiar path on your right. Continue to retrace your steps back to the car park.

4. Back Tor - The Castle Inn

Tel: 01433 620578   Medium - 4 miles - 3hr 30min

This circular walk starts on a quiet lane, and then you will ascend gradually through open countryside to reach Hollins Cross. Continue along a ridge on a good path. You will have wonderful views in all directions. Just as you reach Back Tor, you will descend again in open countryside, with gorse, bracken and scrub amongst the unimproved grassland hillside. There may be livestock and ground nesting birds here, and there is a section of farmland to cross. You will reach the main road through Castleton, but there is a pavement. The pub is reached near the end of the walk. It will take you 1.5 hrs - 2hrs to get to the pub.

How to get there – The car park is off the main road in the centre of Castleton.

Grid Reference – SK 148 829

Postcode – S33 8WP

Parking – Pay and display Castleton National Park Visitor Centre

Facilities – Toilets at the car park

You will need – Dog leads, dog bags

The Walk

❶ Go to the furthest end of the car park (away from the road) and face the stream. Turn right and continue to the corner of the car park. Pass between the bollards and continue beside the stream, with houses on your right.

On reaching another road (Mill Bridge), turn left. Continue on the quiet road. As you leave the houses behind there is a stream on your left, where your dog can get a drink. Ignore a footpath on your left.

Ignore a road on your right, and continue on the quiet lane for some distance. As you continue around a sharp left hand bend, ignore a track on your right (which is signposted as a footpath). **❷** After about half a mile on the quiet lane you will reach a fingerpost and an interpretation panel on your right, go through the gate, and follow the sign on the fingerpost for Hollins Cross. Ascend between the stock fence and hawthorns on a sunken path. At the end of the path there may be livestock, put your dog on a lead, or under close control and pass through a gate.

Ascend to a fingerpost and continue to follow the sign for Hollins Cross, taking the path on your second left. You will ascend into open countryside. On reaching a gate, pass through it and continue to ascend on the obvious

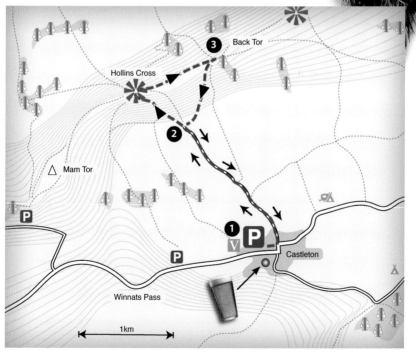

path between the bracken. Continue to ascend, ignoring a footpath on your left. Pass through a gap in a fence line, and continue now on an improved stone slab path.

Ascend the steps, and on reaching the top (Hollins Cross) you will be rewarded with wonderful panoramic views on a clear day. Mam Tor can be seen on your left and Back Tor on your right. Pass through the gate and turn right. Ignore the gate on your right. Continue to ascend, between the stock fence and stone wall. As you continue, you will reach and pass through another gate.

Continue beside the stock fence on your left. Back Tor can be seen straight ahead. Just before you reach Back Tor, you will reach a stile on your left. ❸ Turn right here, and then just after, turn right again on the descending path. Just after, take the path on your left and descend the hillside.

Just before you reach a line of mature trees, take the path which veers to your right. Continue to descend to the line of trees. Pass the trees, with the pine tree on your right, on the obvious worn path. You will soon cross over another narrow path. Continue straight ahead, descending the hillside.

You will pass a stone wall and a stone post on your right. Continue straight ahead. Just after, take the path ahead and to your right (before reaching a gate). There is a steep slope on your left. After a little distance, step down a small rock outcrop and descend at the bottom of the slope, beside a stock fence and dilapidated stone wall.

As you continue, you will reach a familiar fingerpost. Turn left and retrace your steps, descending on the sunken path. Pass through the gate and turn left on the quiet road. Retrace your steps, where you will pass a footpath/track on your left. Continue on the quiet road, and as you reach the houses again, continue straight ahead, ignoring the quiet road on your right, which leads to the car park. On reaching the main road, cross over and turn right. Continue through the village, where you will reach the Castle pub on your left. The main entrance is just off the side road.

On leaving the pub, cross the main road and turn left. Shortly after, turn right into the car park.

"Wine for the ladies?"

5. Hathersage - The Scotsman's Pack

Tel: 01433 650253   Medium - 4.2 miles - 1hr 45min

This is a wonderful walk, starting below Stanage Edge. The scenery is beautiful, and at times you will be surrounded by hillsides in the distance. You will pass through large fields, where sheep may be grazing. For a short part of the walk you will be free of livestock, where you will follow a river in a small wood known as 'The Warren'. **There is one squeeze stile, where dogs larger than a fit Labrador won't fit through, but you could choose to retrace your steps after reaching the pub, which is at the halfway point.** There are some ascents, but mostly they are gradual. There is a short section on a quiet road. You will reach the pub in about 45 minutes.

How to get there – From the main road on the edge of Hathersage village, head in the opposite direction to Hope and turn left on School Lane. Continue on this road, which becomes The Dale. After some distance turn left, and pass a large parking bay on your right. A little further on the road, take a right hand turn. Continue on this minor road, until you see the car park on your right.

Grid Reference – SK 235 838   **Postcode** – S32 1BR

Parking – Hollin Bank car park, pay and display

Facilities – Toilets close to the car park en-route

You will need – Dog leads, dog bags

The Walk

❶ From the car park near to the entrance, face the road and turn left (staying in the car park). Pass beside the vehicle barrier and continue between the stock fence and stone wall. Put your dog on a lead before you reach another vehicle barrier. On reaching the vehicle barrier, turn right. On reaching the road turn left.

You will pass a toilet block on your right, and then take the next footpath and gate on the right. Descend on the footpath, following the sign for Hathersage and Bamford. Descend the steps, and on reaching another path turn right. Continue to descend on a path, which cuts through a steeply sloped forest.

Put your dog on a lead or under close control, and pass through a gate into farmland. Continue to descend on the path. There is a stone wall below on your left. Continue on a level path, as you cross a sloped field. On reaching a gate, opposite a grand castellated house, go through the gate and continue between the stone walls. Ignore a gate on your left and descend the steps and then turn left.

Continue to descend between the stone walls, with the house on your right. Pass between stone gateposts, keeping your

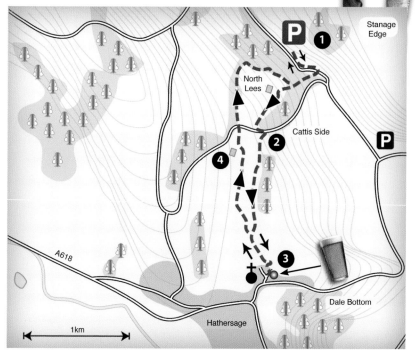

dog under close control or on a lead as there may be livestock grazing. Continue on an access road, with a stone wall on your right and a field on your left. At the end of the access road, go through the gate and turn left on the quiet road. After you have passed a gate on your right, take the next footpath on your right, after about 30 yards, and ascend the steps. ❷ Keep your dog on a lead, or under close control and go through a gate. Continue on a worn path beside a stock fence on your left. The ground slopes away on your right.

Ignore a narrow path on your left, which descends the slope, and continue beside the stock fence. You will reach and cross a track, which leads to a gate on your left. Put your dog on a lead, as there may be free range geese ahead. Continue between the stock fences, with a hedge on your right and a house beyond.

On reaching a gate straight ahead, pass through it and continue straight ahead between the fences. Ignore any gates on your left and right. Ascend a little, where you will gain views ahead and to your right. On reaching another gate pass through it, and continue straight ahead, on the edge of a field. At the end of the field, pass through a gate and continue on the edge of another field. Mature trees line the edge of the field on your right.

At the end of the field, go through the gate and continue on the path. Take a path, which veers slightly to your right and ahead. Descend across a sloped field, with a church ahead of you in the distance. After you have crossed to the other side of the field, descend on the edge of the field, with a hedgerow on your right. In the corner of the field, cross a stone footbridge over a stream, where your dog can get water. Pass through a gate and ascend the steps across a narrow field. On reaching another narrow field, turn right. Continue on the worn path where you will reach and pass through another gate. Continue straight ahead on a quiet road, with the church on your right. At the end of the road you will reach the pub The Scotsman's Pack.

❸ On leaving the pub retrace your steps and ascend on Church Bank. Follow the sign for Parish Church. Ascend on the quiet lane and pass the church on your left. Go back through the gate and continue on the path. As the field begins to widen take the familiar path on your left.

Descend the steps and cross back over the stream via the footbridge. Ignore a footpath on your left, and continue on the familiar path. Ascend on the edge of the field. Don't veer to your right as before, but continue straight ahead on the edge of the field. Descend some steps in the corner of the field, and pass

through the squeeze stones and then the gate. Continue close to the field edge over on your right.

In the corner of the field, on reaching a track, go through the small gate and ascend on the track across the middle of the field. You will reach a gate (often open), pass through the gate and continue on the track in the middle of the field. On reaching a fork, take the lower left path.

At the end of the field, go through a gate and a squeeze stone. ❹ Continue between the fences, where you pass a large house on your left (Brookfield Manor). Pass through a gate, and pass a building on your left. You will pass a stream, where your dog can get a drink. Continue on an access path. On reaching a road, go through a gate, which is on the left of the electric gate. Cross Birley Lane and go through a gate on the opposite side and enter another field.

Continue straight ahead, on the edge of the field. At the end of the field, go through the small gate and enter into a wood, known as The Warren. Continue beside a stream on your left, where your dog can cool off. Go past a bridge on your left and continue to ascend beside the river below.

You will reach and descend some steps, where you will meet the river again. Just after, put your dog on a lead or under close control and go through a gate on your right. Continue straight ahead, and ascend through open countryside. There are boulders and bracken on your left.

Continue on a slightly sunken path and just before you reach a gate turn left and then turn right. Ascend beside the stock fence on your right. On reaching a gate, pass through it and continue straight ahead, beside the boulders and ascend across a field.

Pass through a gate beside the stone wall and continue on the obvious path, where you will descend. Continue straight ahead past a small stone and marker post on a level path, which cuts across the slope. There are views of Stanage Edge ahead. Pass through a small gate (now in a familiar spot) and continue on a track, which cuts across a forest hillside.

Take a path on your left, which ascends the steps. Pass the toilet block, and turn left on the road and retrace your steps to the car park.

6. Mill Stone - The Mill Stone

Tel: 01433 650258   Medium - 4 miles - 2hrs

The walk starts and ends at the pub. There are wonderful views from the beginning. The walk is mostly on the edge of pasture, and you will walk along the River Derwent under the shade of trees. There is a slight gradient across grazing fields with parkland trees, and a quiet track, which is access for a few houses, so there may be vehicles on it. There is a short section of road, and there maybe livestock grazing throughout. There may be ground nesting birds in rough areas of grassland.

How to get there – The Millstone pub is just outside Hathersage, heading towards Sheffield on the main road A6187. The car park is on the right hand side of the road, opposite the pub.

Grid Reference – SK 241 808

Postcode – S32 1DA

Parking – Pub car park

Facilities – None

You will need – Dog leads, dog bags

The Walk

❶ You will need to keep your dog on a lead to begin the walk. From the car park go to the road and turn right. Cross the head of a lane on your right and then ascend beside the road. On reaching another lane turn right into Greenwood Farm. Keep your dog under close control or on a lead, as there may be livestock. Descend between stone walls. You will reach and pass through a gate. Continue to descend on the tarmac path. A stream passes under the path, where your dog can get a drink.

Continue beside a stock fence on your right. There are open fields, with some silver birch and bracken on your left. You will reach a farmyard. **❷** Veer to your right before you reach the stone building. Descend beside a stone wall on your left. There are wonderful views ahead of you.

Pass the end of a stone wall on your right and go around a bend, and then descend with stunning views ahead. Just before you reach a house turn right on the footpath, which is marked by a waymarker. Continue straight ahead, and after about 30 yards turn left, and descend to a gate. Go through the gate and pass through a tunnel under the railway.

Turn right and pass a stream, where your dog can cool off. Continue in an open area, with rocks covered in moss. Veer to

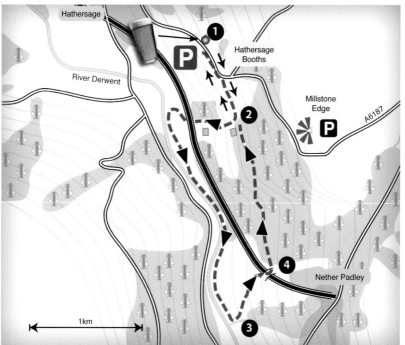

your left, before you reach a gap in a stone wall. Continue beside the stone wall on your right. You will reach an access road. Turn left, where you will continue beside the River Derwent on your right.

Just before you reach a cattle grid, veer to your right and pass through a kissing gate to enter into a large field. Continue straight ahead, beside a stock fence on your left. At the end of the fence continue straight ahead, through the middle of the field.

You will cross over the remains of a stone wall at ground level. Continue straight ahead, with the tree-lined river again on your right. You will reach and pass through a kissing gate and continue straight ahead beside the remnants of a stone wall on your left.

At the end of the field, go through a gate into woodland, and continue beside the river. You will pass over a stream and just after, ignore the footpath on your left and continue straight ahead. At the end of the wood, pass through the gate and continue straight ahead on the edge of a field, and beside the river.

At the end of the field, pass through a gate and continue on the edge of another field. Continue beside the river, and just before you reach the end of

this field, veer to your left. ❸ Pass a stile on your right and turn immediately to your left (before you reach a gate). Continue into a narrow section of the field. Continue beside a stone wall on your left through rough pasture, and ascend on the field edge.

Continue through a large gap in the stone wall. Continue beside the stone wall to your left on the edge of another field. When you reach the corner of the field, you will pass the remnants of an old stone building. Pass between gate posts and enter into another field, where you turn right.

Continue on a raised grass path. Keep your dog under close control or on a lead, as there is a bridge ahead. Cross the railway bridge and pass through a gate. ❹ Turn left on the track and ascend past the houses on your left. The track is an access road for the houses, so listen out for vehicles. Continue straight ahead, where you will enter into rough pasture.

You will reach and continue beside a stone wall on your left. Pass a farmhouse and buildings on your left, and then continue between stone walls. At the end of the walls, continue on a track through the middle of rough pasture. You will pass some old unfinished mill stones on your right.

As you continue, you will pass between stock fences, with oak and silver birch trees beyond. You will pass between gate posts, where you will see a water trough on your right. You will reach and pass farm buildings, now in a familiar spot. Continue straight ahead, and retrace your steps back to the car park and pub. Remember to turn left on reaching the road.

7. Longshaw Estate - The Fox House

Tel: 01433 630374 | Easy - 2.5 miles - 1hr 15min

This walk takes you through the grounds of the Longshaw Estate, which is owned by the National Trust. There are many paths, which are shaded by trees, where your dog can escape the heat on a hot summer day. You will pass through some open areas, and sheep or cattle may be grazing for most of the walk. The pub is located near to the end of the walk. There is a fairly busy road to cross to reach the pub. There are some views across the wonderful landscape. It is recommended in busy periods to book in advance if you want to have a meal at the pub. It will take you about an hour and a quarter to reach the pub.

How to get there – From Hathersage continue on the A6187 in the direction of Sheffield. Turn right following the signs for the National Trust Longshaw Estate. Turn right following the sign for car park and Longshaw Estate visitor centre.

Grid Reference – SK 266800   **Nearest Postcode** – S11 7TY

Parking – National Trust Woodcroft car park pay and display

Facilities – There is a shop/café visitor centre and toilets near to the car park

You will need – Dog lead, dog bags

The Walk

❶ Keep your dog on a lead, while in the estate gardens at the beginning of the walk. From the car park, pass the pay-and-display and an interpretation panel on your left, following the well-made path. Go over a bridge, passing between the stone walls.

On reaching a fingerpost turn left, following the sign for Wooden Pole car park and Estate Office. Ignore a footpath on your left and continue on the path, beside a stone wall on your right, with buildings beyond. Continue straight ahead, where you will pass through a gate (usually open), and then ascend gradually through the wood.

Ignore a narrow path on your right and continue to ascend gently. At the end of the wood, you will reach a gate. Put your dog on a lead, or under close control and pass through the gate into open countryside. Continue straight ahead, on the good surfaced path. The ground slopes away on your right. After some distance the path becomes grass, and soon after it splits into two. Take the lower path, ahead and to your right.

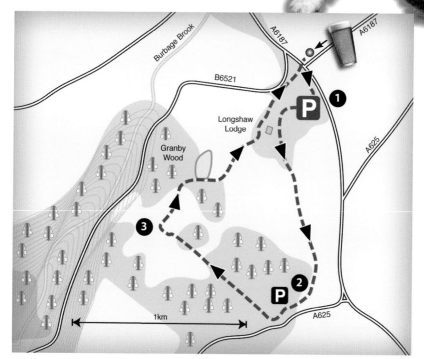

About 100 yards before you reach a road, you will see a path on your right. Take this path and enter into a car park. ❷ Continue through the car park, and on reaching a stone wall on your right, take the path on your right. Continue on the obvious path through the largely spaced woodland carr. Descend gently, and on reaching another path, cross it and continue straight ahead.

Follow the sign for Yarncliff, and you will have views ahead of the hills beyond. You will pass a block of fir/pine trees on your right. Continue to descend gently. A stream passes under the path which you are on, where your dog can get a drink. Here you will begin to ascend gradually. Continue beside a block of mixed broadleaved trees on your left. As you pass the block of trees on your left, you will reach and continue beside a block of fir/pine trees on your right.

Ignore a path on your right soon after, which leads to a gate in the distance. Continue straight ahead, and keep the pine trees on your right. You will reach and pass through a gate, where you will enter into mixed woodland. Continue straight ahead on the obvious path.

❸ On reaching another path on the woodland edge, turn right and ascend gently, beside a stock fence on your left. Pass through a gate and continue on the path, with rhododendron on your right and Longshaw meadow on your left. You will reach and pass a pond on your left. At the end of the pond, continue between rhododendron ascending on the good surfaced path.

Continue to ascend into an open area. On reaching a gate, pass through it and continue on the good path, with a gully on your right. You will reach three

gates and a millstone. Go through the gate on your left. Continue on the path, where you will pass the visitor centre over on your right. There are views on your left, across fields to the hills beyond.

On reaching a sealed track soon after, turn left. Keep your dog on a lead, as this is an access road, and there is a busy road ahead. As you reach a small gate house and an entrance/exit, take the path on your right, and ascend into the wood. Shortly after, ignore a path on your right. Keep your dog on a lead or under close control, as there is a road ahead. Before you reach the road, put your dog on a lead. At the end of the path, pass through an entrance in the stone wall. Cross the road with care, and you will reach the pub on the opposite side. Turn right, and using the narrow path go around to the back of the pub, where you will reach the entrance via the car park.

On leaving the pub, retrace your steps back to the entrance into the wood and Longshaw Estate. Take the path, which is on your immediate left. Continue close to the stone wall on your left, with the road beyond. Keep your dog under close control or on a lead, as there are gaps in the stone wall.

Continue on the edge of the wood, and as you merge with another path, ignore the path on your right. Continue straight ahead, where you will reach the car park on your right.

"Who said I have a beer belly?"

8. Ringinglow - The Norfolk Arms

Tel: 0114 230 2197   Medium - 4.5 miles - 2hr

This is a fabulous walk, starting in a forest called Lady Canning's Plantation. You will cross Burbage moor, where you will reach Burbage Rocks. The views are tremendous, and the scenery is absolutely stunning. The rocks are popular with climbers, and there is a cliff edge, so care must be taken with your dog. There is also the possibility of sheep grazing, and ground nesting birds (end of March to end of July). The walk is not advised in the snow, as the paths will be impossible to see whilst you cross the moor. The pub is reached at the end of the walk.

How to get there – The walk is close to Sheffield, off Ringinglow road. The nearest town in the Peak District is Hathersage. The car park is found close to the junction of Ringinglow road, on Sheephill Road. From Hathersage, continue on the A6187(main road) heading for Sheffield. Shortly after passing the Fox House Inn on your left the road becomes the A625. Continue on the road and turn left at a bend, onto Sheephill Road. Continue on this road, and just as you reach the 30 mph speed limit, turn left into the car park.

Grid Reference – SK 290835   **Postcode** – S11 7TU

Parking – Free in car park (if the car park is full, you can park at the pub at the end of Sheephill road)

Facilities – None   **You will need** – Dog leads, dog bags

The Walk

❶ From the car park, continue in the direction away from the road. Just before the end of the car park, go into the entrance for Lady Canning's Plantation on your right. Keep your dog on the main path, and under close control, as there are cycle tracks within the forest. Continue straight ahead on the main path through the plantation.

Near to the end of the plantation, cross another path, and continue straight ahead. ❷ Go through the gate, cross a path and continue through another gate straight ahead. Keep your dog under close control, as there may be sheep grazing on the moor, and ground nesting birds.

Continue straight ahead on the obvious path through the heather. You will reach an outcrop (two large rocks, named Ox Stones). Turn right and continue, where you will reach another outcrop. Continue past the outcrop on the obvious path. Continue on this path for some distance. There are no distinguishing features, but you will have a road on your right in the distance for some of this section. Continue on the worn path, and you will eventually reach another path.

❸ Turn left on this path. On your right there is a lengthy stretch of rock face (Burbage Edge), with drops below.

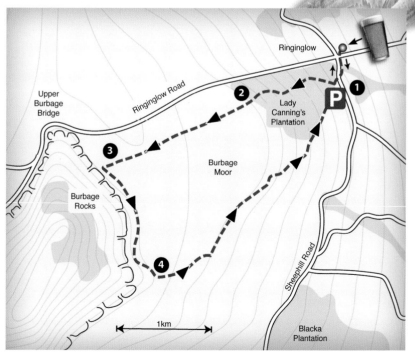

Keep your dog on a lead or under close control. Continue on the worn path, with breath-taking views on your right. The path continues beside the rock face for some distance. The rock face will end, and you will see sloped ground on your right. Continue on the path. You will descend, and cross a small stream where your dog can get a drink (this may dry up in the summer months). Ascend again and continue on the path.

You will eventually reach two cairns (piles of stone/rock), and a fingerpost. ❹ Turn left and ascend through the heathland on the worn path. You will eventually reach a stock fence and a kissing gate. Go through the kissing gate, and continue with the stock fence on your left. On reaching another kissing gate, go through it and on reaching a track just after, turn left. Continue across the moor on the track. This is a byway, so listen out for traffic.

Continue on the byway for some distance, ignoring any paths on your left and right. Eventually you will reach the car park. To reach the pub, continue past the car park. On reaching the road continue straight ahead. At the end of the road you will see the pub on the opposite side of another road.

On leaving the pub, cross over the road and retrace your steps on Sheephill Road. Pass the houses and ignore a footpath on your left. When you reach a sharp bend in the road, leave the road and continue to the car park.

9. Wye Dale - The Church Inn

Tel: 01298 85319   Medium - 7 miles - 3hr 30min

This is an amazing circular walk, with wonderful scenery throughout. You begin the walk in Wye Dale, beside the River Wye. You will also enter the fabulous Chee Dale, cross some stepping stones beside a rock face, and then ascend quite steeply over open pasture and fields, to reach the village of Blackwell. A linear section on quiet road, and then rough grassland brings you to the Church Inn on the edge of Chelmorton. You will retrace your steps, and then descend into the dale via Chee Dale nature reserve, where you will have amazing far reaching views. There are some sections of very quiet road, a busy road to cross, and possibly horse riders and cyclists on a section of path at the beginning and end. There may also be livestock grazing on some sections of the walk. Please book in advance if you wish to have a pub meal. The pub is reached after about 2 hrs. There is a stile with a lift gate for dogs.

How to get there – From Buxton, follow the sign for Bakewell on the A6. After roughly 2.5 miles you will find the car park on your left. The car park is opposite an aggregates entrance (Topley Pike quarry).

Grid Reference – SK 105725

Postcode – SK17 9TE

Parking – Wyedale car park pay and display

Facilities – None

You will need – Dog leads, dog bags

The Walk

❶ From the car park continue away from the exit and join the good surfaced track. Keep your dog under close control as there may be vehicles to access cottages ahead. There may also be cyclists and horses as it is a bridleway. The river Wye is on your left. There is also a narrow path next to the river, which will alleviate some of the possible traffic and cyclists.

You will pass under several viaducts as you continue to follow beside the river. You will see and ignore a footpath on your right, as you approach the third viaduct. Soon after, you will pass a cycle hire cabin on your right, and at the end of the private car park on your left, turn left, crossing the car park. ❷ Cross the footbridge, and turn right immediately afterwards. Pass a cottage on your left, and continue on the path beside the river.

Just before an ascent, take the footpath on your right, and turn left as you reach the river. Continue on the path alongside the river, with a stone wall on your left. On reaching a footbridge, don't cross it, but descend the stone steps on your left. Pass under a viaduct, and continue on the narrow path, where you will pass through a gate. Continue straight ahead on the narrow path. In the summer months you will be amongst dense vegetation (predominantly butterbur). There are scree and rock crags on your left (take care as there is a steep drop beside the river).

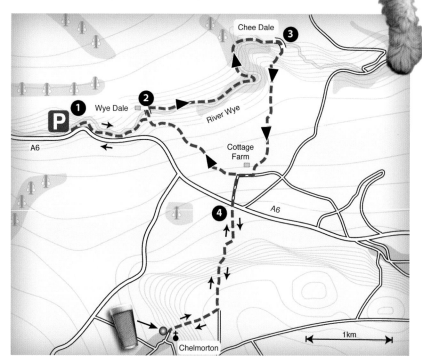

You will reach and cross a stile (there is a gap for dogs), continue under another viaduct. Continue straight ahead, staying beside the river. Again in the summer months there are dense stands of butterbur. Ascend over some rock (steps), and then descend back to the edge of the river. You will have stunning rock face on your left and right, popular with rock climbers.

As the rock face closes in, the path switches to stepping stones next to the rock face on your left. ❸ You will reach and cross a footbridge over the river. Ascend the steps, where you will reach a finger post. Continue to ascend more steps, following the sign for Blackwell Mill.

At the end of the path, put your dog on a lead and go through the gate, where you will reach Monsal Trial, on an old disused railway. Turn right and continue through a tunnel. There may be cyclists, so keep your dog on a lead, or under close control. Soon after leaving the tunnel, take a footpath on your left, signed Blackwell and Chee Dale. Put your dog on a lead and go through the gate. Continue straight ahead, and soon after you will pass beside a gate. Enter a sloped field, and continue straight ahead, on the worn path. Half way across the field, you will reach a finger post. Turn left, following the sign for Blackwell. Continue on the worn grass path, where you will ascend the hill, climbing steeply out of the valley. You will have wonderful views if you look behind you as you ascend.

On reaching a stone wall, go through the gate, and continue straight ahead. There is a stone wall over on your left, and views into the valley on your right. When you reach close to the corner of the field, pass through another gate, and turn right. Continue on the edge of the field, beside a stone wall on your right. At the end of the field, turn right and go through the field gate. Continue on a track beside a stone wall on your left.

You will reach and pass through another two gates on the track. Put your dog on a lead after the second. Continue on the track, where you will pass a farmyard on your right. Continue straight ahead, where you will continue on an access drive. On reaching a quiet road turn right.

Ignore a footpath on your right, and pass Beech Croft Farm on your left. You will pass Beech Croft Farm camp site on your right and just after you will pass Pennine Bridleway on your right, which will be your return route, once you have been to the pub.

Ignore the bridleway for now, and continue on the road. ❹ On reaching a main road, cross over with care, and continue on the access road on the

opposite side. If you let your dog off the lead, keep him under close control, as there may be farm vehicles or vehicles entering the water works ahead.

Ignore the footpath on your left and right, and continue on the road, where you will go around a sharp right hand bend. At the end of the road, go through the gate on your left. Keep your dog under close control or on a lead, as the track will lead to a narrow field, without a gate. Ascend on the track, where you will pass farm buildings on your right. Continue between stone walls, and then ascend through the middle of a narrow field.

In the corner of the field, pass through a gate, and continue straight ahead on a track, between stone walls. On reaching another track go through the second gate on your right, next to a finger post on your right. Follow the sign for Chelmorton. Continue beside a stone wall on your right, through a very narrow field. At the end of the field, descend steeply between the stone walls.

At the end of the path you will reach Church Inn on your right. On leaving the pub retrace your steps until you reach the Pennine Bridleway. After the very narrow field, remember to turn left on the track, following the sign for Chee Dale. Pass again through the narrow field, and continue to the access road. At the end of the access road, cross again with care, and continue on the quiet road opposite. Continue to the Pennine Bridleway, which will be on your left, at the sharp bend in the road.

Take the bridleway, which is signed Chee Dale. Go through a gate and continue on the path between stone walls. Keep your dog under close control, and pass through a gate. Continue on the edge of a field, beside a stone wall. Continue straight ahead, and pass through another gate, into another field. Continue straight ahead. Just after, go through another gate and cross through a small field on a track.

There are amazing, far reaching views. Go through another gate and continue on the edge of a field, beside a stone wall on your right. Cross another track and continue straight ahead, following the track. Go through a gate, and descend into Chee Dale Nature Reserve. Continue on a worn grass path, descending back into the valley, between steeply sloped banks. Ignore a footpath on your right and continue to descend.

Pass through a gate and cross a bridge. Descend and turn right on reaching a finger post, signed for Wormhill. Descend to a familiar spot, and turn left, where you will pass the cycle hire cabin once again. Continue on the path, where you will reach back to the car park.

10. **Monsal Head** - Monsal Head Hotel

Tel: 01629 640250   Easy/Medium - 1.6 miles - 1hr 30min

This is a short circular walk, but there is a fairly steep uphill path through woodland at the end of the walk. At the beginning of the walk you descend through woodland to reach a lovely weir in the valley. The walk continues in the valley, through a meadow alongside the River Wye, in picturesque scenery. You will pass under the impressive Monsal viaduct. The pub is at the start/end of your walk, and dogs are welcome in the Stables Bar. Booking is recommended at weekends and school holidays. Give yourself about an hour and a half to get back to the pub. **There is a squeeze stile and larger dogs won't get through, however there is a bank, and if your dog is agile he will be able to go over the bank to avoid the stile.** There may be livestock.

How to get there – From Bakewell, head in the direction of Buxton. Turn left on the A6020, following the sign for Chesterfield, Sheffield and Ashton in the Water. Shortly after, turn left following the sign for Monsal Head on the B6465. Take the right hand turn (opposite the Ashford Arms), and continue on the B6465. Continue on this road, pass the car park for Monsal Head and continue until you reach another car park and pub on your left.

Grid Reference – SK 188 716   **Postcode** – DE45 1NL

Parking – Pay and display   **Facilities** – Toilets in the car park

You will need – Dog leads, dog bags

The Walk

❶ With your back to the pub and facing the road, turn left and left again. Pass the side of the pub on your left, and the short stay car park on your right. Continue to the sharp right hand bend in the road, where you will have lovely views. Pass through a gap in the stone wall and turn left on the footpath, following the sign on the fingerpost for Ashford/Monsal Dale.

Descend the steps and stay on the lower path, which cuts through the steeply sloped woodland. On reaching a gate, pass through it and continue on the path, descending into the valley.

On reaching the bottom of the valley, you will pass a large pool where a weir has slowed the river. You will reach a gate; keep your dog under close control or on a lead, as the water is fast flowing and there may be livestock and ground nesting birds. Pass through the gate and pass the weir on your right.

Continue on the path beside the River Wye. ❷ On reaching a bridge, cross it and turn right. Continue on the path as you pass through a meadow, beside the river on your right. On reaching a gate, pass through it and continue beside a steep wooded bank on your left. Head towards a viaduct.

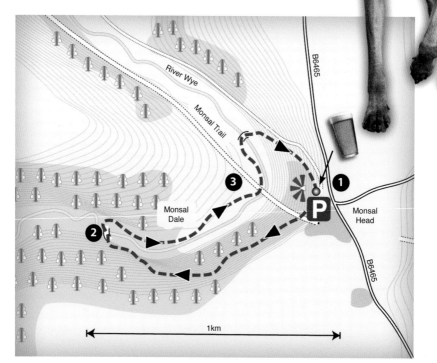

On reaching the viaduct, go through a squeeze stile (if your dog can't fit through, lead him over the bank and go around). ❸ Pass under the viaduct and continue on the path in the valley, with the river on your right. Ignore a footpath on your left and continue straight ahead, where you will reach a bridge.

Put your dog on a lead or under close control and cross the bridge. There are free range hens ahead. Pass a stone barn on your right and then turn right. Continue on the path, which ascends and cuts across a wooded hillside. Keep your dog under close control, as there's a road on your left and there is no boundary fence.

Ignore a footpath on your right and continue straight ahead. Put your dog on a lead and ascend the steps, and then retrace your steps back to the car park and the Monsal Head Hotel.

"I'm always a good girl!"

11. **Rowsley** - The Grouse and Claret Pub

Tel: 01629 733233 | Medium - 5 miles - 2hr

This is a splendid circular walk, which is largely in the grounds of Chatsworth estate, and consists of pasture land with mature parkland trees. There is some woodland and forest plantation, with some heathland and scrub. There is fantastic scenery throughout this walk, and wonderful views. You will reach the pub halfway along, as you enter the village of Rowsley. There is a small section of road, with pavement. There may be cattle on a short section, and sheep may be grazing for most of the walk. **Booking in advance is advised if you wish to have a meal at the pub. Please state that you have a dog, as the dog friendly section is limited indoors.** The pub is about 1hr from start of walk.

How to get there – From Bakewell, take the A6 heading for Matlock. On reaching the village of Rowsley, turn left onto the B6012 following the brown signs for Chatsworth. Continue on this road turning left, following signs for the garden centre and Calton Lees car park.

Grid Reference – SK 258684   **Nearest Postcode** – DE4 2NX

Parking – Calton Lees car park, pay and display

Facilities – None

You will need – Dog leads, dog bags

The Walk

❶ From the car park, go back onto the road and turn right. Pass the entrance for a garden centre on your left. Continue on this quiet road. Near the end of the road turn left, where you see a sign on a finger post for Rowsley. Ascend gently, and on reaching the end of the road, put your dog on a lead or keep him under close control, and go through a gate beside a stone stile. Continue to follow the sign for Rowsley, on a worn path at the edge of a sloping field.

Just before you reach the end of the field, enter into another field via the gateway on your left. Turn right, and continue on the edge of the field with a stone wall on your right to begin with. Descend through the field, with views on your left and ahead of you. There is a wood on your right and there are parkland trees in the field. Continue on the worn path, where you will head towards a gate.

At the end of the field, go through the gate and continue straight ahead on the worn grass path, through the middle of a field. The right of way that you are on is part of the Derwent Valley Heritage Way. You will reach and pass through another gate (sometimes open). Continue on the worn grass path through the middle of the field.

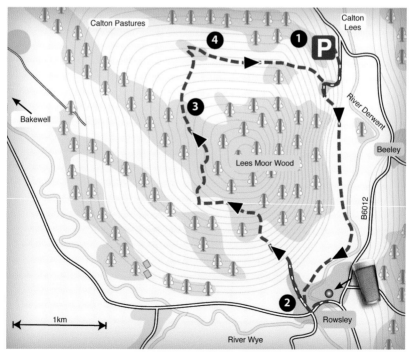

The field will become narrow, with trees on each side of you. Look out for a gate on your right. Go through the gate, following the sign for Heritage Way Derwent Valley. Continue straight ahead, on a path amongst the trees. The path will lead to another gate on the edge of the wood. Go through the gate and enter into another field. The River Derwent is on your left, so check the flow of the water, before allowing your dog to access the river.

Continue straight ahead, beside the stone wall on your right, on the edge of the field. At the end of the field, go through the gate and continue on a track. Keep your dog under close control, as there's access to fields on the bank on your right. You will reach and pass through another gate. Continue straight ahead on the track. As you reach a stone wall on your left, put your dog on a lead. You will pass a church on your far right, and then pass under a viaduct. On reaching a road, turn left. Continue through Rowsley Village. At the end of the road, turn left onto the main road. ❷ Cross over a road bridge, with the River Derwent below.

You will soon reach the Grouse and Claret on your left. Enter the pub at the back, via the side of the car park. Go through the beer garden, and enter the pub. On leaving the pub, turn right on the main road. Turn right on Church Lane. Ignore the footpath on your right (your outbound route), and continue on the road.

You will pass St Katherine's Church on your right. Continue to ascend on the road. At the end of the road, continue straight ahead on the track, where you will soon be between fields. There are views on your left. Ascend gradually and then ascend a little steeper. You will reach two vehicle barriers. Continue on the track you are on, which is signed Bridleway, and pass beside the barrier. You will have amazing views on your left.

At the end of the track, pass beside a vehicle barrier and turn right on another track. Almost immediately, take the bridleway on your right, which is signed Chatsworth on the finger post. Ascend on the path, with mature trees of mainly Ash and Oak. Ascend quite steeply. You will reach and continue on a track on a more gradual ascent.

On reaching a finger post, take the track on your right. Continue to ascend quite steeply on the bridleway, through the forest, with some mature beech trees. As you reach level ground, continue beside a stone wall on your right. You will pass between stone gate posts, and then continue on the obvious path through the forest. Continue through a woodland ride (clearing of trees). Continue on the obvious path. ❸ At the end of the forest, you will pass through two gates in close succession. Keep your dog under close control and continue straight ahead. Descend on an obvious path through a large sloped field, which has blue way markers to guide you. The views are amazing on a clear day.

Descend into the valley, where you will reach a stone wall and woodland beyond it. Continue on the path, which veers to your left. Go through a gate and turn right. ❹ Go through another gate almost immediately, and continue beside a stone wall on your right, with trees beyond. You will reach another path, turn right and pass though the gate.

Descend between the stone walls, keeping your dog on a lead or under close control. Pass between the houses. After you have passed the house on your left, go through a gate on your right, which avoids a cattle grid. Continue on an access track, which zig-zags around the hillside. Continue beside a stone wall on your right. As you continue, as the path levels out, you will pass a water trough on your left, where your dog can get a drink.

The track is lined with trees in places, and there's a stream on your right beyond a stock fence. The field slopes above you on your left. As you continue, you will reach and pass through a gate. Continue on the quiet road, now in a familiar spot. Retrace your steps on the road, where you will reach the car park on your left.

12. Youlgreave to Over Haddon
- The Lathkill Hotel

Tel: 01629 812501   Medium - 7 miles - 3-4hrs

This is a beautiful, mostly linear walk. Those dogs that like the water will love it. For most of the way, you will walk beside the River Bradford. There are many weirs along the way and woodlands on both sides of the river. Flowers blossom on each side of the path in summer, attracting many butterflies and bees. There is a gradual ascent across pasture land to reach the pub. You will cross over some fields, where livestock may be grazing, and there is a short section on a quiet lane, without a pavement. Your dog will have plenty of opportunity to have a drink along the way. **This walk is not suitable for larger breeds of dog, due to a tight squeeze stile. Your dog must also be fit enough to jump onto a small wall (2ft), as another squeeze stile is very narrow.** Roughly 2 hours to the pub.

How to get there – From Bakewell take the A6 heading towards Matlock. Turn right onto the B5056, following the signs for Ashbourne and Youlgreave. Ignore the turn off for Ashbourne and continue. Drive through the village, where you will reach the car park on the right hand side.

Grid Reference – SK 205640   **Postcode** – DE45 1WB

Parking – Payment at the car park

Facilities – Toilets in the car park.

You will need – Dog lead, dog bags

Dog Friendly Pub Walks - Peak District

The Walk

❶ From the village car park go back onto the road, cross over and turn right. On reaching a small green area, with a bench on your left, take the footpath ahead and to the left. Pass through the gate and descend the grassy bank.

You will enter into mixed broadleaved woodland and as you descend a little further, the path levels out and you will reach a river. Dogs will enjoy a paddle here, or a cool drink. Continue on the path beside the river. The path may get a little encroached in the summer months.

On reaching a stone wall, pass through the kissing gate. Turn left on meeting another path, descending towards a stone bridge.
❷ Keep your dog under close control and cross the bridge, ensuring that he doesn't jump over the wall. Turn left, following the river and pass through the weighted gate, on reaching a moss-covered wall.

The river has many different species of aquatic plants, giving colour and texture amongst the clear water. Continue on the surfaced path, with grassy banks, wild flowers and trees on your right, and trees on the other side of the river.

There are several weirs along the river, made of stone walls and earth, that slow the water down, creating a pond-like water body on one side and a flowing river on the other. After a while you will reach a stock

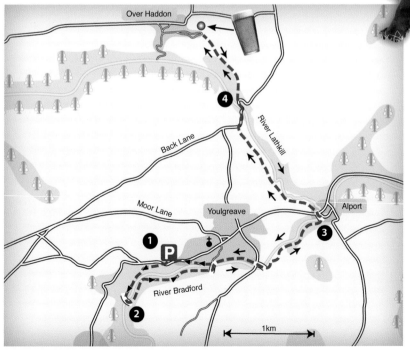

fence on your left, which prevents your dog from entering the water. When you reach a gate on your left, call your dog close and pass through it, then cross the footbridge.

Turn right, put your dog on a lead or under close control and go through the gate, following the river again, with a grass hillside on your left. There may be livestock grazing here. There are lovely, mature parkland trees, with trees surrounding the area.

You will pass another weir, but different from the others, with only a raised wall holding the water back. The water is beautifully clear here, with no vegetation so you can see the bottom of the river bed. Continue along the path and on reaching the gate, put your dog on a lead, pass through and continue straight ahead on the quiet road, beside the cottages on your left.

Just after, cross another road and continue straight ahead, where you reach a gate. Pass through the small gate and continue on a track, beside the river. As you reach a field on your left, the river crosses under the track and is now on your left. There is a rock face on your right. You will pass a pack horse bridge on your left, and continue straight ahead on the track.

As you continue you will leave the rock face on your right, and soon after take the path on your left and ahead. Go through the kissing gate and continue on a good surfaced path, where the river will meander on your left. When you pass a large rock face on your right, keep your dog under close control, as there is a farmyard and access road ahead.

On reaching the gate put your dog on a lead, pass through it, and continue straight ahead on the access road. At the end of the access road you will pass through a gate (often open). ❸ Cross over a road, and continue straight ahead, passing between the squeeze stones if the access gate is closed. Veer to your right, away from the driveway, and continue between post and rail fences.

Pass through a small gate straight ahead, and continue between a stone wall and a stock fence. The river is over on your right. Keep your dog under close control, as at the end of the path there is access into a field, where there may be livestock grazing. Pass between squeeze stones, and continue on the edge of the field. Keep your dog under close control or on a lead, as you will continue to cross a further six fields. Keep to the edge of the fields, and when you reach the last field you will pass a stone house over on your left. At the end of this field, you will cross a lane.

Continue straight ahead (slightly right), and continue on the track between a stone wall and a wire fence. At the end of the track, put your dog on a lead, or under close control. Pass through a small gate, and enter another field. Continue on the obvious path, beside the stone wall on your right. On reaching the end of the field cross a stile (gap for dogs).

Continue between a stone wall and a wire fence. Keep your dog under close control or on a lead, as there is a road ahead, without a barrier. Continue on the path, and where it veers to your right, put your dog on a lead. The path continues beside the wire fence and away from the stone wall. On reaching the road turn right. Continue with care, as there is no pavement.

You will descend on the road, where you cross over the river below. Ascend again, and ignore the footpath on your left. ❹ Continue to ascend for a short distance, and where the road bends sharply to your right, leave the road and continue straight ahead on the footpath. Pass between the squeeze stones, where your dog may jump onto the wall here, as it is very narrow. Continue to ascend, and veer to your right between the trees. On reaching the field boundary, pass between the squeeze stone (dogs may be better on the wall) and then go through the small gate. Keep your dog on a lead or under close control.

Turn left and then continue near to the edge of the field. You will reach a gate on your left. Pass through this and continue across the field, with a steep slope on your left. There are fabulous views ahead and into the valley on your left. Continue on the obvious path, with a stock fence over on your right. As you continue you will be beside the stock fence.

You will reach a gate on your right, marked with a waymarker. Pass through the gate and turn left, but veer slightly to your right, crossing the corner of a field. On reaching a stone wall, pass through two gates, and then cross through the middle of a field, heading for the white building ahead, which is the pub.

At the end of the stone wall, go through the gate and between the squeeze stones. You are now at the end of the road, and at the pub.

On leaving the pub, retrace your steps much of the way back. Keep your dog under close control or on a lead, whilst you cross farmland. Remember to veer to your right across the first field. Pass through the two gates and stay near to the stock fence on your right, veering slightly to your left, to cut the corner off. Pass through the gate, and continue with the stock fence on your left.

Go through another gate, and stay close to the right hand side of the field boundary. Go back through another gate and squeeze stone, put your dog on a lead and descend to the road. Turn right on the road, and descend, and then ascend. Look for the familiar finger post on your left, and continue as before, retracing your steps on the tracks and field edges.

Remember after you have crossed the six fields there is a path between a stock fence and a stone wall, with a busy road at the end. Keep your dog under close control. Near the end of this path, put your dog on a lead, go through the open gate or between the squeeze stones. Cross the road, and continue on the access track as before. Pass the pack horse bridge once again, and continue to the gate. Put your dog on a lead, cross the road and continue straight ahead, beside the river on your left.

The return is a little different on reaching the footbridge. Don't cross the footbridge as before, but cross the end of a road and continue straight ahead. Ignore a path just after on your right. Continue beside the river on your left, and gardens on your right. You will reach and pass through a gate. Ascend on the path between trees.

The path has a series of switchbacks, with some steps. Continue to another gate. Put your dog on a lead, and continue on the narrow path, between stone walls. You will pass beside houses, and after going around a house you will soon reach the road. Turn left on the road, where you will soon reach the car park on your right.

13. The Nine Ladies - The Flying Childe

Tel: 01629 636333   Medium - 5 miles - 2hrs 30min

This is a fabulous circular walk around Stanton Moor, where you will reach a stone circle, known as 'The Nine Ladies'. A detour here will take you to Stanton in Peak, where you will reach the pub. Whilst on the edge of the moor you will have some wonderful views across the countryside. There is a short section of farmland to cross, which leads you to Birchover village. There is a steady ascent through woodland at the end of your walk. There is a stile, with a lift gate for your dog, and there may be livestock, which are used as a grazing tool periodically on the moors. There are some quiet roads without pavements. You will reach the pub after about 45 minutes.

How to get there – From Bakewell, follow the sign for Matlock on the A6. After you pass the car park for Haddon Hall on your right, take the next right hand turn, signed for Ashbourne and Youlgreave. At the bend in the road, turn left staying on the B5056. Take the second left hand turn, following the sign for Birchover. Continue through the village, and stay on the road out of the village. After some uphill bends you will see a car park on your left.

Grid Reference – SK 241 624   **Postcode** – DE4 2BL

Parking – Free in the car park, next to the quarry car park on Birchover Road.

Facilities – None

You will need – Dog leads, dog bags

The Walk

❶ From the car park, go back onto the road and turn left. Pass Birchover Stone Quarry on your right. Continue to ascend gently on the road, where you will pass another quarry entrance. Soon after, take the path on your right, and pass beside stone boulders to enter into Stanton Moor.

Ascend gently between the silver birch trees. You will reach a gate, put your dog on a lead or under close control. Go through the gate and pass an interpretation panel on your left. Ascend beside a stock fence on your right.

There is a heathland bank on your left and you will reach a standing stone, known as Cork Stone. Take the path on your left on reaching the stone, and follow the path, where you pass a quarried area on your left. Ignore the path on your right. After a gradual rise there are lovely views on your left of the surrounding countryside. You pass a trig point on your far right, then another quarried area on your left, which has a drop so keep your dog under close control.

Keep to the well-worn path, where you will have views on your right as you continue. A little further along you will reach silver birch woodland. The path will become a little unclear along the grassy glades within the woodland. Continue straight ahead, where you will see a fence line on your far left. Keep

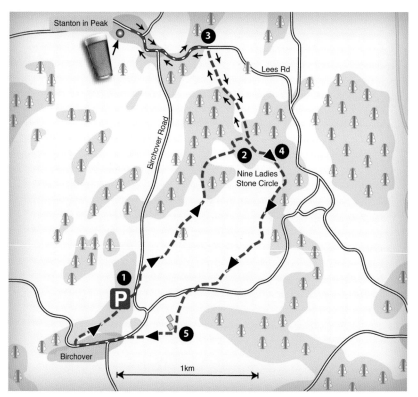

this fence line on your far left, and you will see the path once again a little further along.

You will pass a small stone post on the path, continue straight ahead.

Continue along the path, where silver birch thins out to be replaced with heather and grassland once again. Pass a fenced enclosure at the corner and take the wider path, which veers to your right. The area opens out with a glade and a stone circle, known as The Nine Ladies. Silver birch trees now surround the meadow.

Pass the stone circle on your left, where you will reach another path, and an interpretation panel. ❷ Turn left on the path. Ignore a minor path on your right (this will be the path you take once you have been to the pub). Ignore another path on your right (a fork) just after, and continue on the main path between the widely spaced trees.

You will reach and pass through a gate. Continue on the path beside the stone wall on your right, with woodland on your left. Continue to another gate. Pass through the gate keep your dog under close control or on a lead, as there may be livestock in the field. Cross the field on the obvious path. On reaching the end of the field, put your dog on a lead and go through the gate. ❸ Turn left on the quiet road, listening for traffic, as there are no pavements.

You will descend on the road where you will reach Stanton in Peak village. On reaching another road turn right. Continue to descend through the village. Pass Coach Lane on your right, and continue to descend. Pass Church Lane, and a little further along you will see the pub on your left.

On leaving the pub retrace you steps, ascending back through the village. Remember to turn left on reaching the road which is signed for Stanton Lees. Continue to ascend on the road, and turn back into Stanton Moor, opposite the Block Stone Quarry entrance.

Cross the field, and retrace your steps to just before you reached the Nine Ladies. ❹ Take the narrow path on your left, which was described earlier (about 50 yards before the interpretation panel ahead of you). Continue on this narrow path, where you will reach a stock fence and a stile after about 20 yards. Cross the stile, using the lift gate for your dog.

Turn right and continue on the worn path beside the stock fence on your right. There's a woodland slope on your left. You will pass a tower known as Earl Grey, over on your right.

A little further on you will see a standing stone straight ahead, don't go to the stone, but continue around a right hand bend at the corner of the stock fence. Continue beside the stock fence on your right, with bracken and trees on your left. As you continue you will ascend gently with views on your left.

On reaching a stile on your right, cross this, using the lift gate for your dog.

Turn left on the worn path through the moor. You will reach another path, turn left and descend. On reaching another stile, put your dog on a lead and cross the stile. Turn right on the road, and just after turn left onto a footpath. Continue to a gate. Don't go through the gate, but continue on the path beside the stock fence, with a camp site beyond it. Put your dog on a lead and continue into a courtyard.

Turn left, but stay close to the building on your left and keep the rest of the buildings on your right. Pass Hill Carr Barn on your right, and on reaching a gate don't go through it, but turn right, following the fingerpost sign for Winster. ❺ Continue between the hedge and stone wall. Pass between the squeeze stones, and veer to your right. Pass between another set of squeeze stones and continue straight ahead, following the sign on the fingerpost for Birchover.

Continue beside a field on your left, and then turn left on an access road. Descend to a road. Turn left on the road and descend through the village. Just before you reach The Red Lion pub on your right, take the footpath on your right.

Skirt around a house, and turn left to ascend the steps. Continue to ascend beside a stone wall on your right. On reaching another path, turn right and ascend through the wood. You will see discarded stone slabs, which have been worked on and now left. Continue to ascend on the path, which cuts through the wooded hillside. You will then reach back to the car park.

14. Hartington - Charles Cotton or Devonshire Arms

Tel: 01298 84229 (CC) 01298 84232(DA)   Easy - 3 miles - 1hr 30min

The walk starts at the centre of Hartington. After a section of road you will follow quiet tracks and lanes between stone walls, where you will have views of the surrounding countryside. You will cross farmland and descend to Beresford Dale, which is picturesque with rock faces and the crystal clear River Dove. After an ascent through woodland you will cross farmland, to reach back into the village. There may be livestock. There are some sections of road. The pubs are reached at the beginning or end of your walk.

How to get there – Hartington has the towns of Leek, Buxton, Bakewell, Matlock and Ashbourne all surrounding it. It is reached via the B5054. The walk begins in the centre of the village.

Grid Reference – SK 128603

Postcode – SK17 0AL

Parking – free on the road in the square (triangle)

Facilities – Toilets near the end of the walk

You will need – Dog leads, dog bags

The Walk

❶ From the square, continue on the road and pass the Devonshire Arms on your right. Turn right and ascend on Hall Bank road. Ignore a lane on your right, and continue straight ahead. ❷ You will pass Hartington Hall on your left, and then turn right on Leisure Lane immediately after, following the sign on the fingerpost for Hulme End. Keep your dog on a lead or under close control, as the lane is used for farm vehicles.

Continue between the stone walls, with fields beyond. ❸ Continue around a sharp right hand bend; and put your dog on a lead, as there is a road ahead. On reaching the quiet road turn left, following the sign on the fingerpost for Hulme End. Descend on the road, and then turn right on the lane, which is signed on the fingerpost for Wolfescote Dale.

Ascend between the stone walls, with fields beyond. You will have views across the fields to the hills beyond

on your right. Pass between stone buildings and ascend gently. Ignore a footpath on your right, put your dog on a lead, as there is a road ahead, and continue on the lane. On reaching the quiet road, turn right and descend.

Ignore a footpath on your right, and continue on the road. On reaching a second footpath and fingerpost on your right turn right, following the sign for Hulme End, Wolfcote and Beresford Dale. Pass through a gate and descend between stone walls. Turn a sharp left hand bend and continue between the stone walls. You will begin to descend quite steeply.

When you see a lane on your left, take the footpath on your right. Put your dog on a lead, or under close control, as there may be livestock. Go through the gate, and descend, and shortly after you will be beside a stone wall, on an elevated path on the edge of a field. You will reach Beresford Dale, and on reaching a narrow bridge, cross the river. ❹ Turn right and continue beside the river on your right. There is a wooded slope on your left and moss-covered outcrops on your right, and later on your left also.

On reaching another bridge, cross the river and continue on the path. You will ascend away from the river and then pass through a small wood. On reaching a stone wall, put your dog on a lead. Go between the squeeze stones. Continue straight ahead, on a well-worn path through the middle of a sloped field. Continue to follow the waymarked path.

On reaching a stone wall you will see a water trough, where your dog can get a drink. Go through a small gate and continue on the well-worn path through another field on the well-worn path. On reaching a stone wall, go through a gap and enter into another field.

Continue beside the stone wall on your right for about 50 yards, and then veer to your left, where you will join a well-worn path, which skirts around the bottom of a small hill. Ascend to a stone wall and a gate. Pass through the gate and cross a track. Go through another gate on the opposite side. Continue beside a stone wall on your left. There is a steep slope and crags on your right.

Continue straight ahead on the path, where you will pass through an opening into another similar field. Pass some farm buildings on your left and a farmyard and farmhouse. Descend to a gate, and put your dog on a lead. Go through the gate and descend the steps between buildings. Cross a car park, where you will reach a road. Turn right and continue through the village, where you will reach the car park and the pubs.

Dog Friendly Pub Walks - Peak District

15. Ilam/Dovedale - The Old Dog

Tel: 01335 350990   Medium - 5.4 miles - 2hr 30min

This walk begins at Ilam Country Park. You will cross several fields as you walk alongside the River Manifold. There may be livestock grazing. There are some country lanes to walk on before reaching the Old Dog pub. After the pub, there is a busy road, but there is a pavement. You will reach wonderful scenery in the valley of Lin Dale, and on reaching the river you can cross via the famous stepping stones. The pub has a nice covered courtyard if you choose to sit outside or tables inside, and is reached roughly an hour into your walk.

How to get there – From Ashbourne take the A515 heading towards Buxton. Take a left turn following the sign for Thorpe, Dovedale and Ilam. On entering Staffordshire, follow the sign for Ilam Country Park.

Grid Reference – SK 134 508

Postcode – DE6 2AZ

Parking – Pay and display National Trust car park

Facilities – Toilets in the car park

You will need – Dog leads, dog bags

The Walk

❶ From the car park, go back to the car park entrance. Use the footpath alongside the church to get off the driveway. On reaching the road continue straight ahead, passing houses on your left. Head towards, and then pass a cross on your left. Cross the road bridge with care, as there is no pavement.

❷ Turn left immediately after crossing the bridge, and continue on the footpath, marked by a fingerpost. Keep your dog under close control or on a lead, as there may be livestock. Continue straight ahead on the edge of the field, with the River Manifold on your left.

At the end of the field pass through a gate and cross a footbridge. Continue on the field edge beside the river. There are views on your right. Beware, as when you reach the far corner of the field there is a weir, so keep your dog on a lead if he has a tendency to go in the water. At the end of the field, go through the gate beside the weir and then cross a footbridge.

Continue on the field edge, where you will have lovely scenic views. Near to the end of the field, go through the small gate (20m after you pass the large field gate). Continue straight ahead on the worn path between trees and scrub. The river is now further away on your left.

The path is undulating, and there is pasture on your right beyond the scrub. The path can get boggy in places here. You will pass yellow waymarkers to help guide you. You will reach and continue beside a stock fence on your left. A little further along, just after you leave the fence

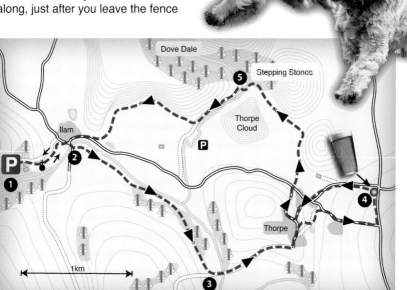

line on your left, the area opens up, where the trees become more sparse. Continue straight ahead on the worn path through the field.

Descend a hill, where you will reach a track. Continue on the track and go through a gate. Ascend a hill and continue straight ahead. You will soon see a gate ahead on your left. Head for this gate, but about 10 yards before you reach it veer left into the scrub. Go through the gap in the stone wall, where you will enter onto a bridge. ❸ Turn left, but keep your dog under close control or on a lead. If your dog has a tendency to jump onto or over walls, there is a drop on the other side.

Continue across the bridge, ignore the footpath on your left and go through the gate straight ahead. Continue straight ahead on the track between stone walls, with fields beyond. At the end of the stone wall you will begin to ascend on the path between fences. There is woodland on your right. When you pass the woodland there are sloping fields on your right with wonderful views. A little further on, ignore a footpath on your left marked by a waymarker. Continue straight ahead. The path will level out and you will have a stone wall on your left. Continue beside the stone wall.

Ignore a footpath on your right just before you reach a gate and houses. Put your dog on a lead and go through the gate. Continue straight ahead on a quiet road beside the houses. Take the road on your right, which is marked by a waymarker and descend on the quiet road, which soon leads to a track. Continue on the track. Pass a track on your right and continue straight ahead, where you will reach a church over on your left. Before you pass the church, take the footpath on your right.

As you continue, ignore a footpath on your right and continue straight ahead. Descend between trees. Ignore another footpath on your right at the end of the stone wall on your right. Continue straight ahead between a short section of post and rail fence. Cross the end of a field and then cross a small footbridge. Put your dog on a lead and ascend to a quiet road.

Turn right and ascend on the road. Pass the houses, and a little further on, pass a farmyard and buildings. Ignore any footpaths and continue to the end of the road. At the end of the road turn left, making use of the narrow grass verge. ❹ After about 100 yards you will reach The Old Dog pub on your left.

On leaving the pub turn left, and then turn left again at the end of the pub. Continue on the road, and pass the pub car park on your left. Continue on the road for quite a distance. When you reach Thorpe Cottage on your left take care, as you will have to walk for a short section on the road. Pass a road on your left. On reaching a second road on your left (signed for St Leonard Thorpe Church) take it. At the end of the quiet road turn right. Continue on Digmire Lane and then through the quiet village.

At the end of the road you will reach a busy road. Cross this road and continue straight ahead into a car park. You will pass a toilet block on your left. Continue to the end of the road and go through the gate straight ahead. Continue straight ahead on the track and pass through open pasture, with many hills ahead.

About 20 yards before you reach a danger sign and a small quarry face, veer to your left. Descend on a worn grass path, through the middle of the valley. There are danger signs on your far right. On your far left there is a pointed peak. When you reach close to the bottom of the valley keep to your left. You will have a stone wall and a stock fence on your left. Continue close to the stock fence and descend deeper into the valley, between sharply sloping hills.

As you continue the steep hillsides will close in. Continue straight ahead, where you will pass exposed rock on your right. On reaching the gate straight ahead, pass through it. Descend to a path. With the river straight ahead turn left and then cross the stepping stones over the river on your right. **❺**

Turn left and continue on the sealed path through stunning scenery beside the river. Go through a gate, beside the cattle grid. Continue straight ahead, ignore a bridge on your left and continue on the path.

Shortly after, take the footpath on your right, which is signed alternative path to Ilam. Ascend the slope and go through a gate. Continue between hawthorns and stay close to the stock fence on your left. Ascend on the worn grass path. There is exposed limestone on your right, and wonderful views on your left.

You will reach and go through a small gate straight ahead. Continue on the edge of the slope, beside a stone wall on your left. The path is fairly level. You will reach and pass through another gate. Continue straight ahead crossing the slope on the worn grass path. Continue beside the stone wall on your left. Pass a footpath over a stile on your left, and just after, ignore a path which ascends. Continue beside the stone wall on your left as you continue around a bend.

At the end of the stone wall you will reach another path. Turn right on this path and continue. About 30 yards before you reach a building ahead, take a narrow path on your left, which descends to a road. Put your dog on a lead, and on reaching the gate, go through it and turn right on the road. You will reach the riverside and Ilam village once again.

You will reach the cross at a familiar spot. Cross the road (just before going over the road bridge), and turn right. Retrace your steps back to the car park.

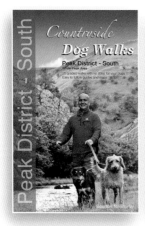

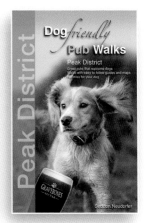
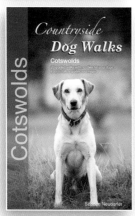
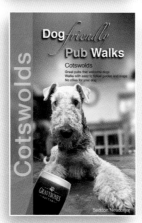
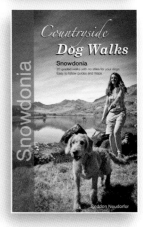
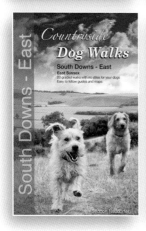
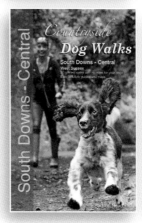
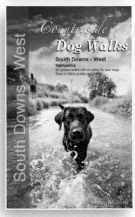

www.countrysidedogwalks.co.uk

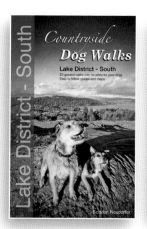

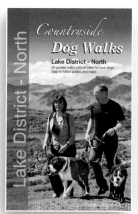

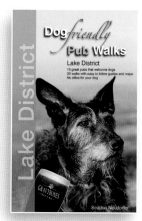

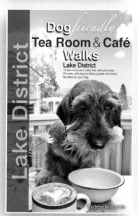

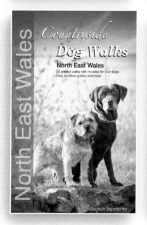

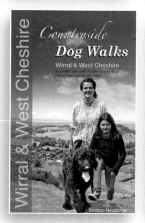

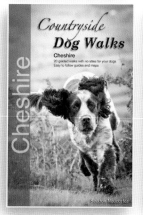

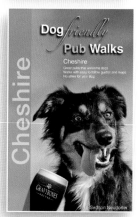

Follow us on Facebook for progress reports on our future publications.

Search - Countryside Dog Walks

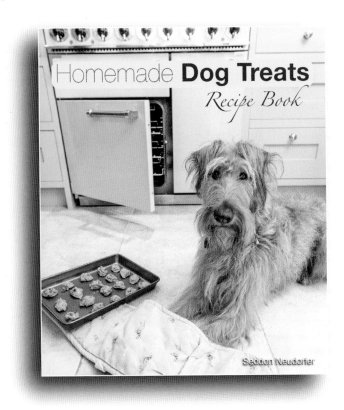

Homemade **Dog Treats**
Recipe Book

Seddon Neudorfer

Simple recipes made from ingredients in your kitchen

Healthy ingredients to ensure a healthy dog

Fun and easy to make

Wet Nose
Publishing Ltd

"Cooking treats is easy"